A Champion...

Born with Autism

Alma Doe

Illustrated by Kalina Dones

I dedicate this book to my grandchildren.

On March 29, 2001 a baby was born to the proud parents of Moses & Deliah Jenkins.

His mother always said, "If it's a boy, I'll name him "Champion."

His father agreed and they named him Champion Moses, "Champs" for short.

IT'S A BOY!

One day, after Champion's 3rd birthday, his parents noticed a difference in their son.

After a month of seeing the same behavior, they called the doctor. They explained their concerns and the doctor made an appointment for Champs to see a Specialist.

After the tests were completed, his parents received the final report. He told them, "Mr. & Mrs. Jenkins, your child has autism."

This was shocking news, but soon afterwards, they agreed they would continue to raise him with the plan and purpose God had for his life.

CHAMPION
DR.

At age 4, Champ's parents found the perfect school for him to attend, and he was so excited!

Right away, he loved his teacher, Ms. Smith. He also liked the other children and he especially liked the colorful classroom.

However, Ms. Smith noticed that at playtime, Champ did not mingle with the other children. He just played alone.

"Champ, is something wrong?" she asked.

Champ did not answer. He just continued playing by himself. Ms. Smith tried assigning him to a group, but he still played as if he were by himself.

MS. SMITH'S CLASS
Welcome
SCHOOL IS FUN!!
A
B
C

As days went by, Ms. Smith noticed how good Champ did on his schoolwork and how attentive he was. Champ completed every assignment from start to finish. She noticed that after only a few weeks of music classes that Champ was very good at playing the piano. He often played one of his favorite songs...

"What would I do without you Jesus
How could I make it through one day

Without Your love to lead and guide me
Without you Lord to show the way

For your will always be my hero
And I will praise and worship you

For You alone, You are so worthy
Hallelujah, bless Your name"

At the first PTA meeting, Ms. Smith told Mr. & Mrs. Jenkins how well Champ played the piano and how he completed all his assignments.

She told them that Champ would not want to go outside and play with the other children. Instead, he would sit and stare out the window facing the playground.

Ms. Smith didn't know that the reason Champ didn't want to play outside was because the other children would make fun of him and bully him.

One night, Dad walked outside on the front porch and saw Champion sitting on the steps. He was crying. He went over to him and asked, "Champion, what's wrong?"

With tears in his eyes, Champion replied, "the kids in school are always saying bad things to me."

"Like what?" asked his father.

"They call me four eyes. They tease me 'cause I don't have a girlfriend. I tell them 'I don't need a girlfriend because my mom's my friend and she is a girl'. Then they call me a mama's boy."

"Oh son, I'm so sorry, Kids can be mean sometimes," said Dad.

"They even make fun of my name" said Champion. "Why did mom give me the name Champion? I'm not a Champion. I'm not good at anything, especially sports!" he said.

At that moment, his father picked him up and placed him on his shoulders. "That's not true!" he exclaimed. "Your report card has nothing but E's on it and that stands for excellence. I can think of so many other things you are good at. Things like chess, checkers, reading, math and science. But most importantly, you are a great son!"

At that moment, Champ also hears a greater voice. It was the voice of his heavenly father and with so much peace and love, He said to him, "You are my Champion, Every purpose and plan I have for you shall come to pass. Your mother only named you what I placed in her heart. Don't worry about what others think of you. Soon, they will all see who you are to me. Through me, you will achieve your goals and destiny... for you are my little Champion!"

Champion learned that day that everyone is special in the eyes of God and that everyone is created with a plan and a purpose.

He became a famous pianist, an award winning scientist and a champion at chess.

With God's help and the love and support of his parents, he accomplished all his goals and dreams.

He was truly a "Champion" just a God designed!

#1
CHAMPION

Champion was the victim of "bullying" at school.

Bullies make fun of others because it makes them feel better about themselves. They act that way because they have low self-esteem and have fear in their lives. Bullies draw crowds to feel important. They don't think about their actions or the consequences that will follow.

Their problems make them need attention, a need to dominate and force control over others. They live in a false fake world and are unhappy and very troubled.

Are you a bully? Ask God to help you stop. He can make you feel better about yourself.

If you stop being a bully you just might become a good friend.

Alma Doe is available for speaking engagements and public appearances. For more information contact:

Alma Doe
C/O Advantage Books
P.O. Box 160847
Altamonte Springs, FL 32716
info@ advbooks.com

To purchase additional copies of this book or other books published by Advantage Books call our order number at: 407-788-3110 (Book Orders Only), or visit our bookstore website at: www.advbookstore.com

Longwood, Florida, USA
"we bring dreams to life"™
www.advbookstore.com